Animal Symmetry

A butterfly

flew into Zoe's garden.

The butterfly opened its wings.

"The butterfly's wings look the same,"

said Zoe.

"They have lines and spots

in the same places."

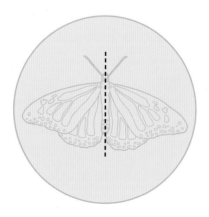

A fat caterpillar was eating a leaf.

"This caterpillar has two long feelers at the front.

They are the same size," said Zoe.

"It has two short feelers at the back.

They are the same size, too."

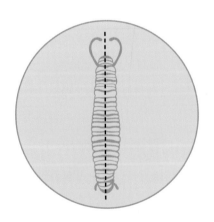

A yellow bee was looking for food in the flowers.

Bzzz ... bzzz ... bzzz!

"A bee has two big wings and two little wings," said Zoe.

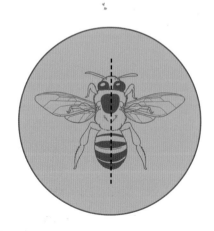

Zoe saw a black and yellow spider sitting on its web.

"Spiders have four legs on one side, and four legs on the other side," she said.

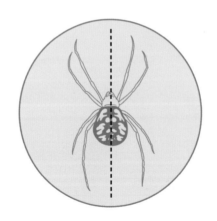

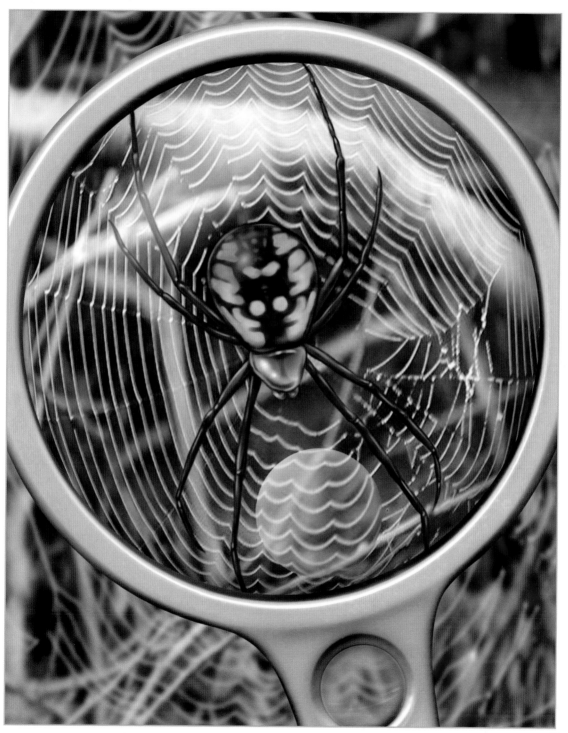

A big brown beetle was on a log.

"The beetle has six legs,

two feelers,

and two eyes," said Zoe.

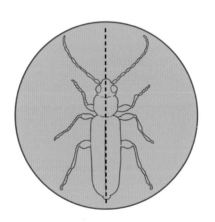

Zoe said, "This grasshopper

has lines and spots

on its legs and its back.

The lines and spots look the same

on both sides.

The colours look the same

on both sides, too."

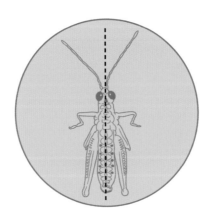

A lizard ran out of the grass.

"This lizard has big round eyes," said Zoe.

"It has lines down its back and spots on its tail."

"Some animals have patterns
on their heads,
their backs,
their legs,
and their wings," said Zoe.

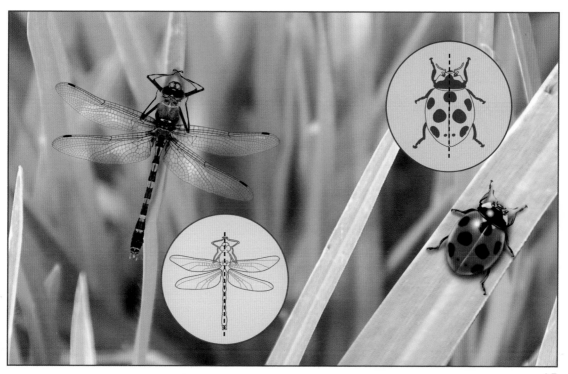

Look again at the **symmetrical** patterns on the small animals in Zoe's garden.

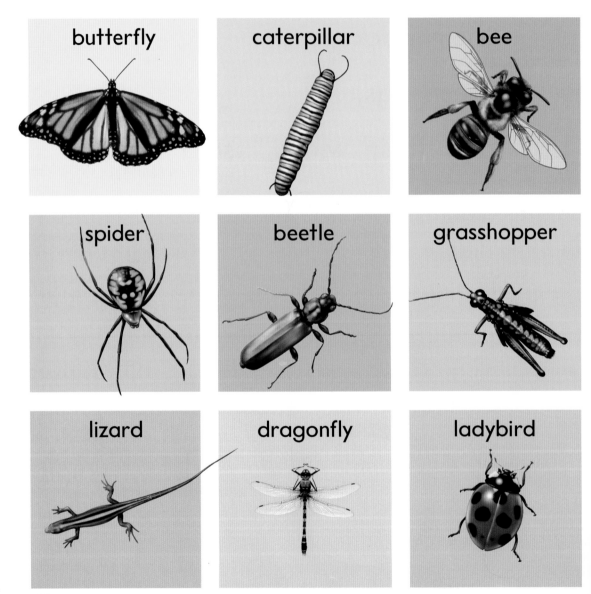

butterfly

caterpillar

bee

spider

beetle

grasshopper

lizard

dragonfly

ladybird